THE FALL FEASTS

Activity Book

The Fall Feasts Activity Book

Copyright © 2019. All rights reserved

This Activity Book may not be reproduced in whole or in part in any manner without written permission from Bible Pathway Adventures.

ISBN: 978-1-98-858538-3

Author: Pip Reid

Illustrator: Thomas Barnett

Creative Director: Curtis Reid

For free Bible resources and Teacher Packs including coloring pages, worksheets, quizzes and more visit our website at:

www.biblepathwayadventures.com

◇◇ INTRODUCTION ◇◇

Enjoy teaching your children about Yom Teru'ah (Day of Trumpets), Yom Kippur (Day of Atonement), Sukkot (Feast of Tabernacles), and Shemini Atzeret (The Last Great Day) with our Fall Feasts Activity Book. Packed with fun worksheets, puzzles, crafts, and coloring pages, plus a handy answer key to help parents and educators just like you teach kids a Biblical faith.

Bible Pathway Adventures helps educators and parents teach children a Biblical Faith in a fun and creative way. We do this via our illustrated storybooks, Teacher Packs, and printable activities – available for download on our website www.biblepathwayadventures.com

Thanks for buying this Activity Book and supporting our ministry. Every book purchased helps us continue our work providing Classroom Packs and discipleship resources to families and missions around the world.

The search for Truth is more fun than Tradition!

✦◇ TABLE OF CONTENTS ◇✦

Introduction 3

Day of Trumpets (Yom Teru'ah)
Introduction: Day of Trumpets 7
Bible coloring page: Blow the Shofar 8
Bible Word Search Puzzle: Day of Trumpets..9
Crossword: Day of Trumpets 10
Bible Quiz: Day of Trumpets 11
Creative Writing: Day of Trumpets.. 12
Coloring activity: Where does a shofar come from? 13
Coloring activity: Day of Trumpets... 14
Fun worksheet: Yom Teru'ah 15
Let's Draw!: Honoring the Day of Trumpets 16
Maze: Help the shofar sounder 17
Write your own story: Birth of Yeshua 18
Word scramble: Yom Teru'ah 22
Bible worksheet: The Sabbath 23
Learning Hebrew: Yom Teru'ah 24
Worksheet: The Day That No Man Knows 26

Day of Atonement (Yom Kippur)
Introduction: Atonement (Yom Kippur).. 27
Bible coloring page: The High Priest 28
Bible Quiz: Day of Atonement 29
Bible Word Search Puzzle: Day of Atonement 30
Bible Word Search Puzzle: Holy of Holies.. 31
Fact Sheet: Repentance... 32

Jonah unit

Write your own story!: Jonah 33

What's the Word?: Prayer of repentance 37

Bible Quiz: Jonah and the Big Fish 38

Bible Word Search Puzzle: Jonah and the Big Fish 39

Bible verse copywork: Jonah repents 40

Fun worksheet: Jonah 41

Learning Hebrew: Yom Kippur 42

Coloring activity: The Torah 44

Maze: Help the High Priest 45

Bible Quiz: The High Priest 46

Worksheet: High Priest's Breastplate 47

The Tabernacle: Label the furniture 48

Fact Sheet: Holy of Holies 49

Color 'n fill-in-the-blanks activity: Repentance 50

Fun worksheet: Yom Kippur 51

Creative writing: Day of Atonement 52

Feast of Tabernacles (Sukkot)

Introduction: Tabernacles (Sukkot) 53

Bible coloring page: My Sukkah 54

Bible coloring page: The Tabernacle 55

Bible Quiz: Sukkot 56

Bible Word Search Puzzle: Sukkot 57

Fact Sheet: The Temple 58

Question 'n color activity: Solomon dedicates the Temple 59

Map activity: Solomon's Temple 60

Fun worksheet: Sukkot 61

Learning Hebrew: Sukkot 62

Coloring activity: Camp of Israel 64

Coloring page: Happy Sukkot! 65

What's the Word?: Celebration! 66

Bible Verse Copywork: Sukkot 67

Word scramble: Sukkot 68

Coloring activity: Decorate your own Sukkah 69

Coloring activity: Marriage supper 70

Test your knowledge!: Sukkot review 71

The Last Great Day (Shemini Atzeret)

Bible Quiz: The Millennial Reign 72

Bible Word Search Puzzle: The Last Great Day 73

Bible activity: Life in the Millennial Reign 74

What's the Word?: Yeshua will rule 75

The Millennial Temple diagram 76

Bible Quiz: Ezekiel's Temple 77

Fun worksheet: Shemini Atzeret 78

Bible activity: The Last Great Day 79

Coloring activity: Judging the Twelve Tribes 80

Coloring activity: What a lot of animals! 81

Bible verse copywork: Ezekiel 82

Maze: Feast of Tabernacles 83

Fun worksheet: Last Great Day 84

Crafts & Projects

Bible Craft: Make your own shofar 86

Bible activity: Who said it? 87

Worksheet: Day of Trumpets 89

Bible activity: Who said it? 91

Worksheet: The Water Ceremony 93

Bible activity: Who said it? 95

Answer Key 97

Discover more Activity Books! 102

DAY OF TRUMPETS

The Day of Trumpets is one of Yah's Appointed Times and is usually celebrated during the month of September. This Day is a Sabbath and people honor this Appointed Time by blowing a shofar (a ram's horn) and making grain and drink offerings. They also use this Day to examine their own behavior and draw closer to Yah.

One of the key themes of the Day of Trumpets is kingship. Did you know the Day of Trumpets was a time to anoint kings? And the Parthian Magi (Wise Men) were known as the "king-makers"? The Hebrew Mazzaroth (the sun, moon, and stars) and scripture appear to confirm the Day of Trumpets as the true birthday of Yeshua. Many people believe Yeshua (our King) will return for His Bride on this Day, at the last trump (1 Thessalonians 4:15-18 and 1 Corinthians 15:51-52).

How do you honor the Day of Trumpets?

....

Do your own research. Do you believe Yeshua was born on the Day of Trumpets? If so, why?

....

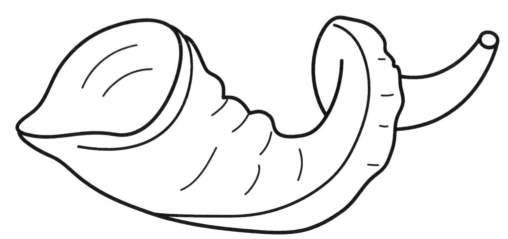

BLOW THE SHOFAR

DAY OF TRUMPETS

Read Leviticus 23, Numbers 29, and Nehemiah 8.
Find and circle each of the words from the list below.

```
H W I D P T K N E A J O B A E W V E L Q
C B B E L S R Q C F E G J J N N H I J G
Y O D J B P O U T B U R N T V L N S J Q
D H N S I N J X M R J S D E R B W R O S
R B P V E C A I A P F Z H I A R Z A E M
R Q U G O N W H D F E F B O T M Z E Y V
E F O L T C H D Q Y G T K N F K X L F P
S R A M I G A K C X W R A C B A C X R Z
T X V V N O T Q S L L N E I B R P B W
U O Y U B D S L I C Q T L H F C N J L R
N X D L I K Z T R O J T Q N T L F Y O H
T Y K O D H X X R Z N D X P V A H V W M
Z S A U I Q B E A U X A L C X M B X I O
T Z J H I Y N E B Y C H W W Q B P E N R
M M X G W C S F Q J H T O O H S M F G O
C T W S T E T I S H R I I L X E W S O F
Q G Q P W F H F X Z Q X F O Y D I J B I
S E T A P A R T P F X H N X N D J H W R
R R L Y K M F O F A O N L T B S U D G E
J D K O F F E R I N G H M Q J C V H E L
```

SHOFAR   TRUMPET   FIRE   REST
HOLY   INSTRUCTIONS   YAHWEH   OFFERING
CONVOCATION   SET APART   BURNT   ISRAEL
LAMBS   RAM   BLOWING   TISHRI

DAY OF TRUMPETS

Read Leviticus 23, Numbers 29, and 1 Corinthians 15.
Complete the crossword below.

ACROSS

4) Which month shall you observe the Day of Trumpets?
5) Day of Trumpets is also known as the Day of _____.
6) The Day of Trumpets is announced using this instrument.
8) "You shall observe a day of solemn _____."
9) "For the shofar will sound and the _____ will be raised."
10) A shofar is made from a _____ horn.

DOWN

1) Yah's appointed times all point to Whom?
2) How do you say Day of Trumpets in Hebrew?
3) On what day of the month shall you observe Yom Teru'ah?
7) "You shall present a _____ offering to Yah."

DAY OF TRUMPETS

Read Leviticus 23, Numbers 29, and 1 Corinthians 15.
Answer the questions below.

1. In which Hebrew month is the Day of Trumpets? ....

2. What instrument is blown on the Day of Trumpets? ....

3. What should you not do on the Day of Trumpets? (Leviticus 23:25) ....

4. On the first day of the _____ month you shall have a holy

   convocation. (Numbers 29:1) ....

5. What type of burnt offering did Yah ask the Israelites to

   make in Numbers 29:2-6? ....

6. What other type of offering is mentioned in Numbers 29:6? ....

7. Which people does Yah want to honor these Feasts? (Leviticus 23:1) ....

8. What two Appointed Times come after the Day of Trumpets?

   (Leviticus 23:26-44) ....

9. "Moses declared to the _____ the appointed feasts of Yah."

   (Leviticus 23:44) ....

10. When will Yeshua return? (1 Corinthians 15:51-52) ....

DAY OF TRUMPETS

Read Leviticus 23:24-25, Numbers 29:1-6, Nehemiah 8:2-6, and 1 Corinthians 15:52. What facts did you discover about the Day of Trumpets? Write a paragraph about this Appointed Time. Use your imagination to color the illustration at the bottom of the page.

WHERE DOES A SHOFAR COME FROM?

Open your Bibles and read Leviticus 23:23-25. Color the picture.

During the Day of Trumpets, a shofar (traditionally made from a ram's horn) is blown 100 times. This Day is also called Yom Teru'ah, which means "Day of Shofar Blasts" in Hebrew.

DAY OF TRUMPETS

Read Leviticus 23:23-25. Fill in the Blanks. Color the picture.

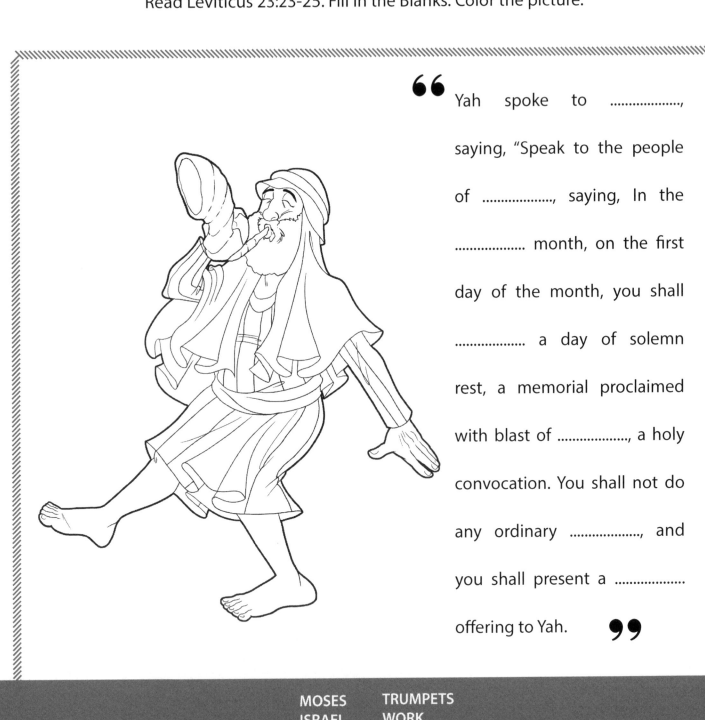

" Yah spoke to ...., saying, "Speak to the people of ...., saying, In the .... month, on the first day of the month, you shall .... a day of solemn rest, a memorial proclaimed with blast of ...., a holy convocation. You shall not do any ordinary ...., and you shall present a .... offering to Yah. "

MOSES   TRUMPETS
ISRAEL   WORK
SEVENTH   FOOD
OBSERVE

Yom Teru'ah

Draw the ancient Israelites honoring the Day of Trumpets.

Design your own shofar.

This Appointed Time teaches me...

Our family keeps this Appointed Time by...

LET'S DRAW!

Draw your family or congregation honoring the Day of Trumpets.

What do you do on this Day?

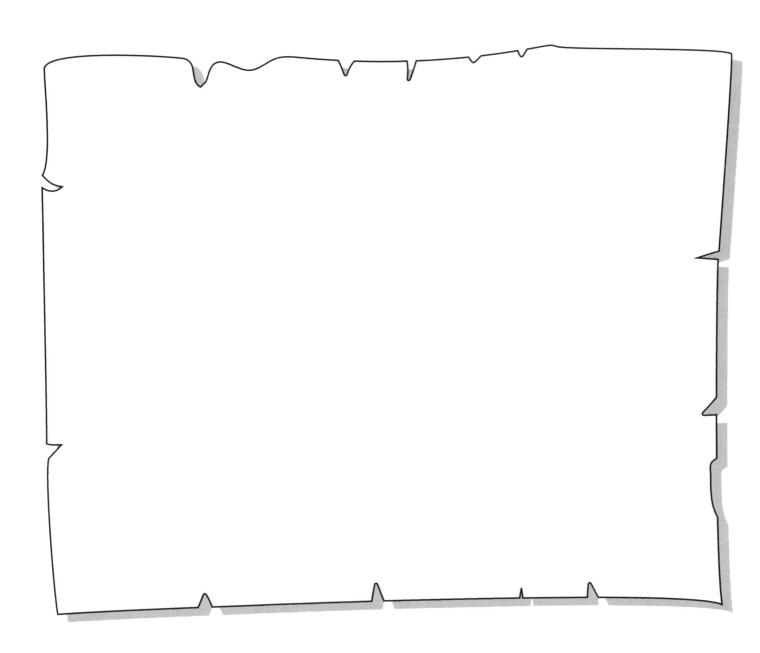

THE SHOFAR SOUNDER

Help the shofar blower find his shofar so that he can announce the Day of Trumpets.

WRITE YOUR OWN STORY!

The Mazzaroth and scripture point to the Day of Trumpets as Yeshua's birthday.
Beside each picture, write this story in your own words. Color the picture.

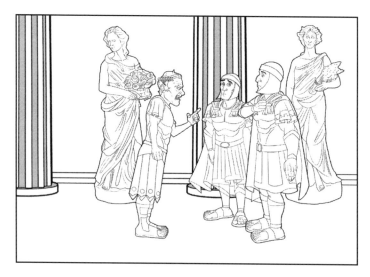

· ·

· ·

· ·

· ·

· ·

· ·

· ·

· ·

· ·

· ·

· ·

· ·

· ·

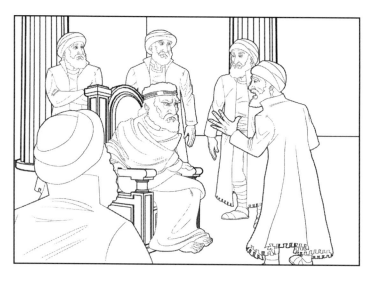

....

....

....

....

....

....

....

....

....

....

....

....

....

....

YOM TERU'AH WORD SCRAMBLE

Unscramble the letters from the words below.

1. SRHAOF: ....

2. YHEUSA: ....

3. YDA: ....

4. ETILEASRI: ....

5. TSE AARTP: ....

6. TSBLA: ....

7. MOY URETAH: ....

8. SETR: ....

SHOFAR   SET APART
YESHUA   BLAST
DAY   YOM TERU'AH
ISRAELITE   REST

The Sabbath

Yom Teru'ah is a Sabbath. Read Leviticus 23:24 and write the Bible verse below.

....

....

....

1. What does Yah tell us to do on the Sabbath? (Deuteronomy 5)

....

....

2. What day did Yah tell His people to keep holy? (Exodus 20:8)

....

....

3. How many days can Yah's people work each week? (Leviticus 23:3)

....

....

Draw what you do on Yom Teru'ah.

What could the Sabbath teach me?	On the Sabbath I…
....	....
....	....

✦ YOM TERU'AH ✦

The Hebrew words for Day of Trumpets are Yom Teru'ah.
The ancient Israelites used to anoint kings on this day.

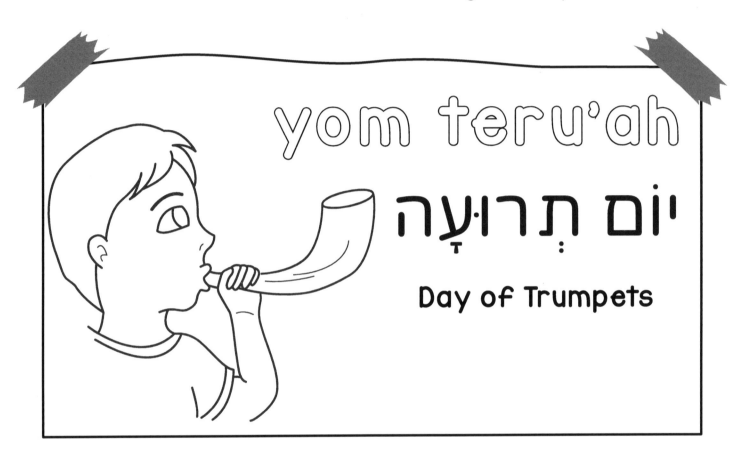

yom teru'ah

יוֹם תְּרוּעָה

Day of Trumpets

יוֹם תְּרוּעָה

LET'S WRITE!

Practice writing these Hebrew words on the lines below.

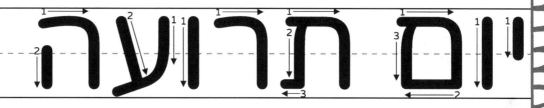

יוֹם תְּרוּעָה

Try this on your own.
Remember that Hebrew is read from RIGHT to LEFT.

THE DAY THAT NO MAN KNOWS

The Israelites knew the Day of Trumpets as 'The Day That No Man Knows.' Why was Yom Teru'ah nicknamed by this Hebrew Idiom? This is the only Appointed Time that is determined by the sighting of the new moon. So, 'no man' can calculate the exact day or hour when it begins.

In ancient Jerusalem, two witnesses stood on the city wall and watched for the first sliver of the new moon. When they saw the new moon appear in the sky, they blew the shofars. Everyone in Jerusalem stopped what they were doing and ran to the temple to celebrate the Day of Blowing (or Yom Teru'ah).

Color the shofar blower

shofar ➡

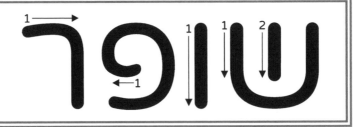

Practice writing the Hebrew word 'shofar' on the line below.

שׁופֿר

∾≈≈≈≈≈≈≈≈≈≈ DAY OF ATONEMENT ∾≈≈≈≈≈≈≈≈≈≈≈

The Day of Atonement is also known as Yom Kippur and is part of Yah's prophetic Appointed Times. It takes place ten days after the Day of Trumpets. On this day we do no work and are instructed to gather together with like-minded believers. It is a time to repent and turn back to Yah and to follow His instructions.

"…The tenth day of this seventh month is the Day of Atonement. Hold a sacred assembly, deny yourselves, and present a food offering to Yah. Do not do any work on that day… This is to be a lasting ordinance for the generations to come…" (Leviticus 23:27-31).

Yah was so serious about this Appointed Time that He asked His people to afflict themselves for one day. Some people honor this Day by not eating (fasting). Many Bible scholars believe the Day of Atonement points to the actual return of the Messiah.

The Bible says that Paul and the disciples still kept the Appointed Times after Yeshua's death and resurrection, including Yom Kippur and Unleavened Bread. How do you honor the Day of Atonement?

"Since considerable time had been lost and it was already unsafe for a voyage, because Yom Kippur had already come and gone, Paul gave them this suggestion…" (Acts 27:9)

THE HIGH PRIEST

These are the garments they are to make: a breastpiece, an ephod, a robe, a woven tunic, a turban and a sash. They are to make these sacred garments for your brother Aaron and his sons, so they may serve me as priests.

(Exodus 28:4)

DAY OF ATONEMENT

Read Leviticus 16.
Answer the questions below.

1. Who was the first high priest? ....

2. What holy garments did the high priest wear in the Holy

   of Holies? (Leviticus 16:4) ....

3. What did the high priest do before he put on the holy garments? ....

4. What happened to the goat on which the lot fell on Azazel? ....

5. Where did the High Priest sprinkle the bull's blood? ....

6. For whom did the high priest make atonement? (Leviticus 16:32-33) ....

7. Who entered the Holy of Holies with the high priest on the

   Day of Atonement? ....

8. Who was Aaron's brother? ....

9. On what day and month is the Day of Atonement? ....

10. What did Yah instruct us to on the Day of Atonement? (Leviticus 16:31) ....

DAY OF ATONEMENT

Read Leviticus 16:17-29, 23:26-27, and Hebrews 9:7.
Find and circle each of the words from the list below.

J D T A B E R N A C L E F E N K C K S V
R C J A J B D G I S R A E L I T E S F H
Q G O O W Q O W F K L S A B B A T H H O
W Q Y F N Q E U P T S Y P V W F G H W I
F I Q S R A F F X E A E S V V K D M R F
Q Y E O N C H U N M W A M I H G P D A W
N L Q Y G C D E E P P O O O Z E O H P C
B A Y G V G X V O L R O O J S W R I P H
V N D Y B M B O H E R T V T D E I G O W
I H T B P N I A K R Y P K L Y U S H I E
Q X E A I P G O Q R L C G C O J U P N Z
L V O B N O M Q F D I B Y V M I P R T N
L D O G R G G C L B N J B D K D T I E J
A D S M D E X R S F C D F B I U C E D Y
A X F N B G W Y A H W E H I P F C S T H
A T O N E M E N T D U Y J C P W L T I D
X F E U M R T J X X J Q S I U K M J M M
R E P E N T A N C E O G D K R C W N E V
J A Y B U R N T H Y T Q S Z J K B H N W
W A T E R L Q C I H H Y E S H U A R I C

ISRAELITES	MOSES	YOM KIPPUR	BURNT
WATER	ATONEMENT	REPENTANCE	YAHWEH
HEBREW	TEMPLE	SABBATH	YESHUA
HIGH PRIEST	JONAH	TABERNACLE	APPOINTED TIME

www.biblepathwayadventures.com
The Fall Feasts: Activity Book

HOLY OF HOLIES

Read Exodus 36-39.
Find and circle each of the words from the list below.

```
M U U T Z L X J Q F N A R U M I R Z S Y
G T K G V O I S R A E L I T E S O S K O
R Q A V W L K G Z A A X B N X A L N M S
R O L B L H K P F T U Z L H U S N X E B
Y B C E E F O F Q C A D O I V H J Q R W
G L A S V R O H L W V B E K R O W S C G
O R L D O I N O J A K D L E R W O D Y V
R Q F Y O N T A G F Z X E E H B G X S T
H H O K V X O E C W I Z Q O R R Y P E W
I O H F U Z I F B L B N Z X B E O S A T
G I M E N O R A H S E J C A Y A M Y T B
H T U I V U U M D X T E K W C D K E T L
P F W Y W J Y J U L H J E B U B I G E O
R X L U M J E I X W O Z C V Z A P B M O
I U U O Z D P I L L A R S C V E P A P D
E W V H I Y X T J K F V K U Y P U Z L I
S W E F O T J A H S J X O T N C R O E T
T H I J Z X Z P C O V E N A N T A O S X
X M L C M O M I L A T O N E M E N T B J
E V O A L T A R Q Z U W J M A U S H Z E
```

SHOWBREAD	HIGH PRIEST	ATONEMENT	TABERNACLE
PILLARS	MERCY SEAT	TEMPLE	ISRAELITES
BLOOD	TABLE	YOM KIPPUR	COVENANT
MENORAH	ALTAR	VEIL	LEVITE

REPENTANCE

What is repentance? Repentance means turning towards the Father and His Ways. The Hebrew word for repentance is Teshuvah, which means turning – turning from self to our Creator, the God of Abraham, Isaac, and Jacob. In Acts 26:20, Paul says, "I preached that they should repent and turn to Yah and prove their repentance by their deeds". In the story of Jonah, the Ninevites wore sackcloth to show Yah they had repented. This was a coarse, black cloth made from goat's hair that was worn with burnt ashes as a sign of repentance. But although the Ninevites repented after Jonah preached, their children didn't follow Yah's ways. One hundred years later, the prophet Nahum warned that Yah would destroy Nineveh because the people were so wicked. Sure enough, Nineveh was completely destroyed by the armies of the Median and Babylonian empires in 612 BC.

What does repentance mean?

....

What did the Ninevites do to show Yah they had repented?

....

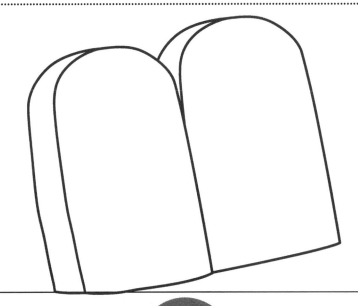

WRITE YOUR OWN STORY!

Beside each picture, write in your own words the story of Jonah. Color the picture.

....

....

....

....

....

....

....

....

....

....

....

....

....

....

....

....

....

....

....

....

....

....

....

....

. . . .

. . . .

. . . .

. . . .

. . . .

. . . .

. . . .

. . . .

. . . .

. . . .

. . . .

. . . .

. . . .

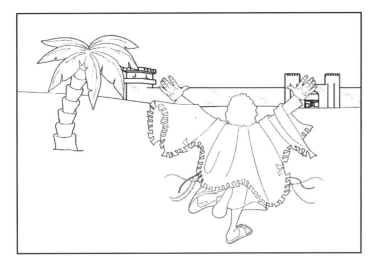

....

....

....

....

....

....

....

....

....

....

....

....

....

....

....

PRAYER OF REPENTANCE

Read Jonah 2:1-10. Fill in the blanks with the words below.

" Jonah prayed to Yah from the belly of the fish, saying, I called out to Yah out of my ..

........................, and He answered me. Out of the .... I cried

and You heard my voice. You threw me into the sea and the waters surrounded me;

Your powerful .... splashed over me. Then I said, 'I am driven

away from Your sight; yet I will look again upon your holy ....'

The sea water closed over me to take my life. The deep surrounded me - seaweed

wrapped around my head. I went down to the land whose bars closed upon me

forever; yet You brought up my life from the grave, Oh Yah my Elohim. When my

life was fading away, I remembered Yah and prayed to You, into Your holy temple.

Those who .... useless idols forsake their hope of steadfast love.

But with thanks, I will sacrifice to You; what I have vowed I will pay. ....

belongs to Yah!" Yah spoke to the .... and it vomited ....

out upon the dry land. "

DISTRESS	WORSHIP
GRAVE	SALVATION
WAVES	FISH
TEMPLE	JONAH

JONAH AND THE BIG FISH

Read Jonah 1-4.
Answer the questions below.

1. To which city did Yah ask Jonah to take His message of repentance? ....

2. Where did Jonah try to run to instead of going to Nineveh? ....

3. In which city did Jonah board a ship? ....

4. What happened after the boat set sail for Tarshish? ....

5. Who threw Jonah overboard? ....

6. What happened after Jonah was thrown overboard? ....

7. How long was Jonah inside the fish? ....

8. What did Jonah do while he was inside the fish? ....

9. How did Jonah get out of the fish? ....

10. What did Jonah tell the people when he reached Nineveh? ....

JONAH AND THE BIG FISH

Read Jonah 1-4.
Find and circle each of the words from the list below.

```
C T J I Q Q U A P O I W M Q V M P Z D D
S B M O A P P M U E P X F F I N R W W I
W H C C N U Y H V R A M G W P N O M I S
Q I E J L A J F J S Q G S N B M P I L T
P T S O O B H Y I X X A A J P X H O A R
F R G R L Y T H O S I H I O R R E O G E
B Q A F A H F C G Z H G L C A D T V P S
S W K Y O E N S W B N B O I B K J P W S
Q X E R E G L D Y X D W R I S L R P X H
I F P Z G R A I R A I J S G M E D T L N
Z A M N J X H C T Z B T M A G S A Y D K
O W M R I R W Q R E P E N T W J U V Y V
R A Z Q D J O R S V R O S B B K I N G D
L W L M Q U U L S L H C H U T L U Y G R
O T D V T N Q O N W J B I Q B E B O P X
L F S M I C G Y C U Y N P Q P E U X F H
E O V E R B O A R D P H H F G S L V L B
X O K J O P P A O C T Q E T A W U L K Q
X K W R L Z I R F G Y X Q J Q X R Q Y D
L N I N E V E H P T V N Q S E W C F J E
```

JONAH REPENTS

Open your Bible to Jonah 3:1-3. Copy the scriptures on the lines provided.
Use your imagination to color the illustration at the bottom of the page.

Jonah

Imagine you were stuck inside a fish for three days and nights. What would you say to Yah?

What did Jonah eat while he was inside the fish? Use your imagination!

Repentance is...

Draw Jonah inside the big Fish.

 YOM KIPPUR

The Hebrew words for Day of Atonement are Yom Kippur.
On this day, the High Priest went into a special room in the temple called the Holy of Holies.

yom kippur

יוֹם כִּפּוּר

Day of Atonement

LET'S WRITE!

Practice writing these Hebrew words on the lines below.

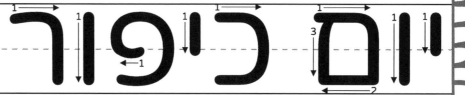

יום כיפור

Try this on your own.
Remember that Hebrew is read from RIGHT to LEFT.

✿✿✿✿✿ THE TORAH ✿✿✿✿✿

Read the Bible verse. Color the picture.

Your Torah is a lamp to my feet and a light to my path.

Psalm 119:105

THE HIGH PRIEST

Help the High Priest make his way to the temple.

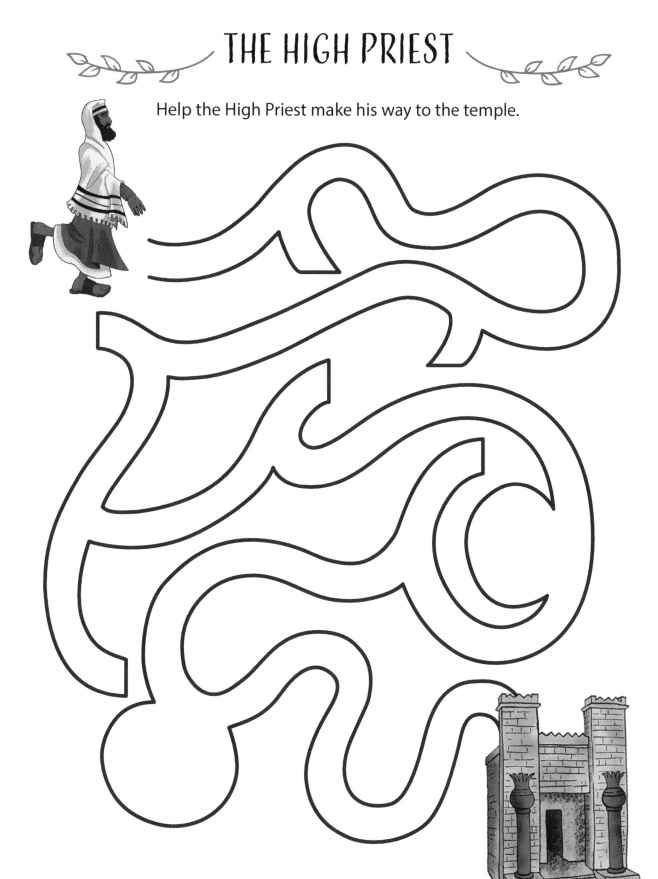

THE HIGH PRIEST

Read Exodus 28, Leviticus 23, Numbers 29,
1 Chronicles 6, 2 Chronicles 22, 1 Kings 2,
John 18, Luke 3, and 1 Corinthians 15.
Answer the questions below.

1. Who was the first High Priest? ....

2. What color was the High Priest's robe? ....

3. On which day of the year could the High Priest enter the

    Holy of Holies? ....

4. What relation was Annas to Caiaphas? ....

5. Yeshua was a High Priest after the order of which ancient king

    mentioned in Psalm 110? ....

6. Yeshua was led away to which High Priest first? ....

7. The wife of which High Priest rescued the infant Joash? ....

8. How many stones did the High Priest's breastplate contain? ....

9. During the reign of King David, who was the High Priest? ....

10. Zadok, the High Priest during the reign of Solomon,

    was of which tribe of Israel? ....

HIGH PRIEST'S BREASTPLATE

Read Exodus 28:21 and Revelation 7. Each gemstone on the High Priest's breastplate represents one of the Twelve Tribes of Israel. Write the names of the twelve tribes of Israel on the lines below. Color the breastplate.

1. ....
2. ....
3. ....
4. ....
5. ....
6. ....
7. ....
8. ....
9. ....
10. ....
11. ....
12. ....

THE TABERNACLE

Read Exodus 36-39. Label the furniture in the Tabernacle. What part of the Tabernacle did the High Priest enter once a year to make atonement for the people?

a) Holy of Holies

b) Veil

c) Altar of Incense

d) Table of Shewbread

e) Ark of the Covenant

f) Menorah

g) Laver

h) Brazen Altar

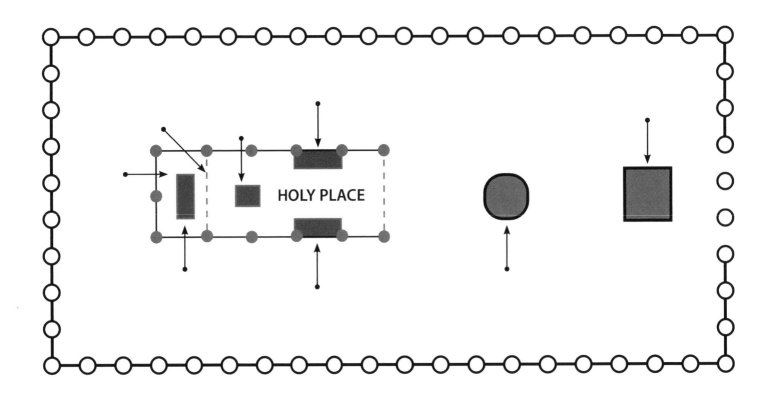

HOLY OF HOLIES

For followers of Yeshua, Yom Kippur is a special day. It's a day to rest and think about our spiritual life – and if necessary, turn back to the Father and His Ways. In ancient Israel, the Day of Atonement was a day when the gift of forgiveness was given to the Israelites. The High Priest made an animal sacrifice and the animals' blood covered their sins symbolically before Yah.

After the temple was built in Jerusalem, the High Priest would go inside a special room called the Holy of Holies, and present an offering to Yah to symbolize a request from the Israelites for forgiveness. The High Priest would then tell the Israelites if Yah had forgiven them and covered their sins. Yeshua is the greatest High Priest - He offered His own body before Yah. His blood now covers all our sins, gives us eternal life, and gives us a way back into the House of Israel.

"But now in Yeshua you, who once were far away have been brought near by the blood of Christ." (Ephesians 2:13)

After the temple was built, how did the High Priest ask forgiveness for the sins of Israel?

....

....

Who is our High Priest today?

....

....

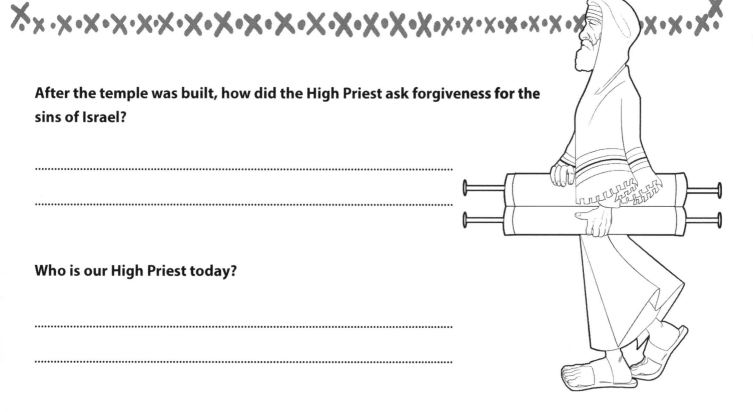

REPENTANCE

Open your Bibles and read Acts 26:20. Fill in the blanks. Color the picture.

66 But I declared first to those in

...., then in

Jerusalem, and throughout

...., and

also to the nations that they

should ....

and turn to Yah, performing

deeds in keeping with their

.... 99

DAMASCUS
JUDEA
REPENT
REPENTANCE

Yom Kippur

Draw the High Priest in the Holy of Holies on Yom Kippur.

If the Day of Atonement was a book, the cover would look like this...

The Day of Atonement teaches me...

I honor Yom Kippur by...

DAY OF ATONEMENT

Open your Bible to Leviticus 23:27. Copy the scripture on the lines provided.
Use your imagination to color the illustration at the bottom of the page.

FEAST OF TABERNACLES

The Feast of Tabernacles (Sukkot) is one of Yah's Appointed Times and is observed during the week starting on Tishrei 15 - usually in late September to mid-October.

"...On the fifteenth day of the seventh month, Yah's festival of Tabernacles begins and lasts for seven days. The first day is a sacred assembly; do no regular work....celebrate this as a festival to Yah for seven days each year. This is to be a lasting ordinance for generations to come; celebrate it in the seventh month. Live in booths for seven days: all native-born Israelites are to live in booths so your descendants will know that I had the Israelites live in temporary shelters when I brought them out of Egypt." (Leviticus 23:34 – 44)

Sukkot begins five days after the Yom Kippur and starts and ends with a special High Sabbath. During this Feast, many people live in temporary shelters (sukkahs) to remind them that Yah delivered the Israelites out of Egypt. In traditional Jewish circles, all meals are eaten in a sukkah and parts of the roof are left uncovered so the stars can be viewed at night. Is this perhaps so people can see God's plan of salvation written in the heavens?

In biblical times, many important events took place during Sukkot. Solomon's Temple was dedicated to Yah (1 Kings 8:2), the Israelites gathered together to hear Ezra proclaim the Word of God (Nehemiah 8), and Yeshua said, "If anyone thirsts, let him come to me and drink. He who believes in Me, as the Scripture has said, out of his heart will flow rivers of living water." (John 7:37–39)

As a part of Yah's prophetic Appointed Times and plan of salvation, Passover, Unleavened Bread, First Fruits, and Pentecost were fulfilled with the death and resurrection of Yeshua. The Fall Feasts of Trumpets, Atonement, and Tabernacles have not yet been fulfilled and speak of His return to collect His Bride. In particular, Sukkot points to the wedding of Yeshua to His Bride.

MY SUKKAH

THE TABERNACLE

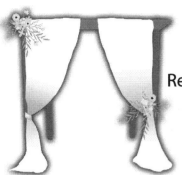

SUKKOT

Read Leviticus 23, Numbers 29, Deuteronomy 16, Zechariah 14, and 1 Kings 8:2-21.
Answer the questions below.

1. How long did Yah tell people to keep the Feast of Sukkot?

2. How many days is Sukkot?

3. On which Feast are people told to live in booths (sukkahs)?

4. When does Sukkot start?

5. What did Yah tell people to do during Sukkot?

6. At what time of the year does Sukkot take place?

7. On what days during Sukkot are people instructed to hold a sacred assembly?

8. Which historical event in the book of Exodus does Sukkot remind us?

9. Which Old Testament king dedicated the temple during Sukkot?

10. How will Yah punish the nations for not keeping Sukkot during the Millennial Reign? (Zechariah 14)

SUKKOT

Read Leviticus 23, Numbers 29, Deuteronomy 16, Zechariah 14, and 1 Kings 8.
Find and circle each of the words from the list below.

```
W A T E R D Y M F T U C Q V D X E U R Y
M F C Q T K A J C E K R N R W W O R A S
I O F B W A R A Z V L F T L I O G V I E
E L X I Q G B T I R H L V N U T E N T C
W H U N Z X I E U U A W O E I E P I D I
O W D H D Y Y P R U F K Y W W E I S P R
H R E V Y Z B A E N M Y B F S J N P I O
P S S D A L W C E R A O F P S H P L L B
M O V Z D J V G Z U Y C S C J L I G G K
Q Y R P K I R F B B A A L E D P I P R D
S X J S C Q N Z G F H I F E S T W S I Y
L S R P A G L G M Z W K Y H S Z Z U M O
F U B J Y B B F F I E W J T M A C K A F
X K G M A X B X H E H V Q U Y P E K G F
I K K F T A S A L O A L N J F S Y A E E
K O Z L P E C B T B L S R W Z S O H D R
U T F Y E S H U A H R R T F U Z Y H F I
H B W H M J V T D E U T E R O N O M Y N
S E V E N D A Y S U L N H A R V E S T G
I Q K L J F S Q T M D G T K E B E D E O
```

OFFERING	YESHUA	SABBATH	TABERNACLES
TENT	HARVEST	SUKKOT	WEDDING FEAST
WATER	SUKKAH	FELLOWSHIP	SEVEN DAYS
PILGRIMAGE	YAHWEH	DEUTERONOMY	MOSES

THE TEMPLE

One of the reasons King Herod enlarged the Temple Mount was to accommodate the huge numbers of pilgrims coming to Jerusalem for the three pilgrimage Feasts: Unleavened Bread, Shavuot, and Sukkot. It took 10,000 men ten years just to build the retaining walls! When they had finished, the platform was big enough to hold twenty-four football fields.

People could only go into the temple courtyards and not inside the temple structure. It was in the courtyards where Yeshua taught the people. The temple was still considered a public building even though its interior was not open to the public. It was also the meeting place of the Jewish Council, the Sanhedrin, the highest court of Jewish law during the time of Roman rule.

Write a reason why King Herod enlarged the Temple Mount.

....

In which part of the temple did Yeshua teach?

....

What was the Sanhedrin?

....

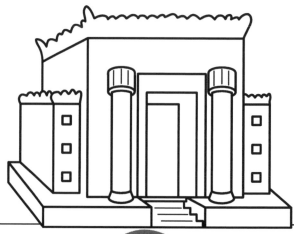

KING SOLOMON DEDICATES THE TEMPLE

Open your Bibles and read 1 Kings 8.
Answer the questions. Color the picture.

1. In what month does the Feast of Tabernacles take place? (verse 2)

....

....

....

....

2. Where did the priests put the Ark of the Covenant? (verse 6)

....

....

....

....

3. How many sheep, goats, and cattle did Solomon sacrifice? (verse 63)

....

....

....

....

SOLOMON'S TEMPLE

Read 1 Kings 6. While Solomon was king, he built a magnificent temple in Jerusalem.
Label the places in the temple from the list below.
You may need to do some research to find the answers.

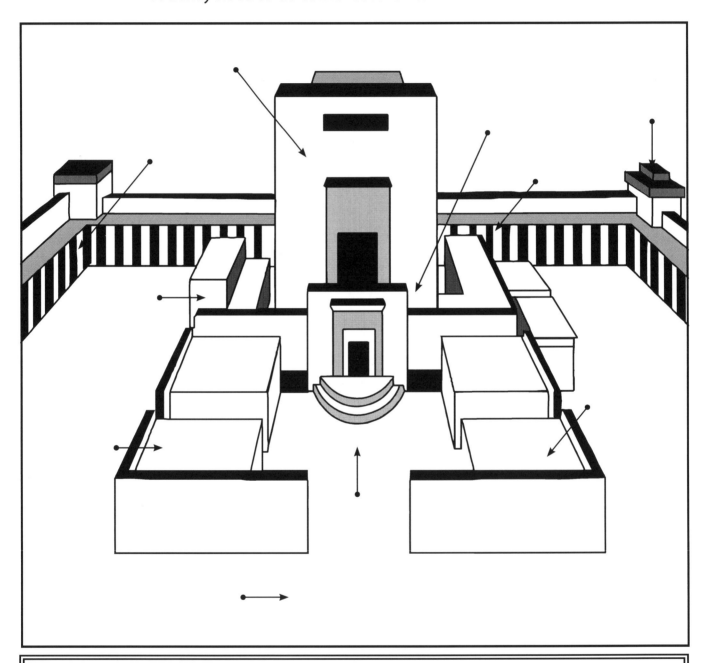

| Levites quarters | Sacrificial wood | Court of the Women | Court of the Priests | Watch Tower |
| Priests quarters | Court of the Israelites | The Holy Place | Solomon's Porch | Nazarites |

Sukkot

Draw your own Sukkah.

If the Feast of Tabernacles was a book, the cover would look like this...

I honor Sukkot by...

This Feast teaches me...

★ SUKKOT ★

The Hebrew word for Feast of Tabernacles is Sukkot. It is one of Yah's Appointed Times and begins on Tishrei 15 - usually in late September to mid-October.

sukkot

סֻכּוֹת

Feast of Tabernacles

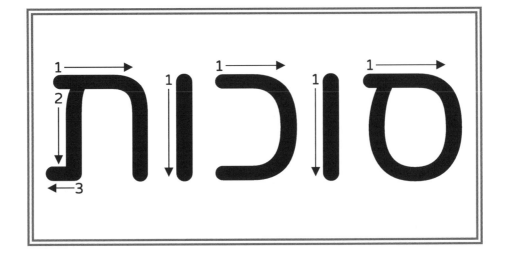

LET'S WRITE!

Practice writing these Hebrew words on the lines below.

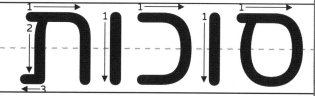

סוכות

Try this on your own.
Remember that Hebrew is read from RIGHT to LEFT.

CAMP OF ISRAEL

Read Numbers 2. The Israelites camped in the wilderness for forty years.
Below each tent, write the name of a tribe of Israel. Color the tents.

Happy Sukkot

CELEBRATION!

Read Nehemiah 8:13-18. Fill in the blanks below.

❝ On the second day, the heads of fathers' houses of all the people, the priests and the ...., came together to Ezra the scribe to study the words of the Torah. They found written in the .... that Yah had commanded by Moses that the Israelites should dwell in booths during the feast of the .... month, and that they should proclaim it in all their towns and in Jerusalem, "Go out to the hills and bring back .... of olive, wild olive, myrtle, palm, and other leafy trees to make booths, as it is written." So the people went out and brought them, and made .... for themselves, each on his roof, and in their courts and in the courts of the house of God, and in the square at the .... Gate and in the square at the Gate of Ephraim. And all the people who had returned from the .... made booths and lived in them. From the days of Jeshua the son of Nun to that day, the people of Israel had not done so. And there was great rejoicing. Day by day, from the first day to the last day, Ezra read from the Torah. They kept the feast seven days, and on the eighth day there was a .... assembly, according to the rule. ❞

LEVITES   CAPTIVITY
TORAH   SOLEMN
SEVENTH   BOOTHS
BRANCHES   WATER

SUKKOT

Open your Bible to Leviticus 23:42-43. Copy the scriptures on the lines provided.
Use your imagination to color the illustration at the bottom of the page.

SUKKOT WORD SCRAMBLE

Unscramble the letters from the words below.

1. SEOSM: ....

2. BSHTOO: ....

3. GNIREFFO: ....

4. WEART: ....

5. SEHCBRAN: ....

6. SEAFT: ....

7. VEENS SYDA: ....

8. DDINEGW: ....

SEVEN DAYS	WATER
OFFERING	BRANCHES
WEDDING	FEAST
MOSES	BOOTHS

DECORATE YOUR OWN SUKKAH!

Have fun decorating your Sukkah. Common sukkah decorations include colorful flowers, fruit, vegetables, palm branches, gourds, Indian corn, lights, artwork, bunting and lanterns. Use your creativity and color the page!

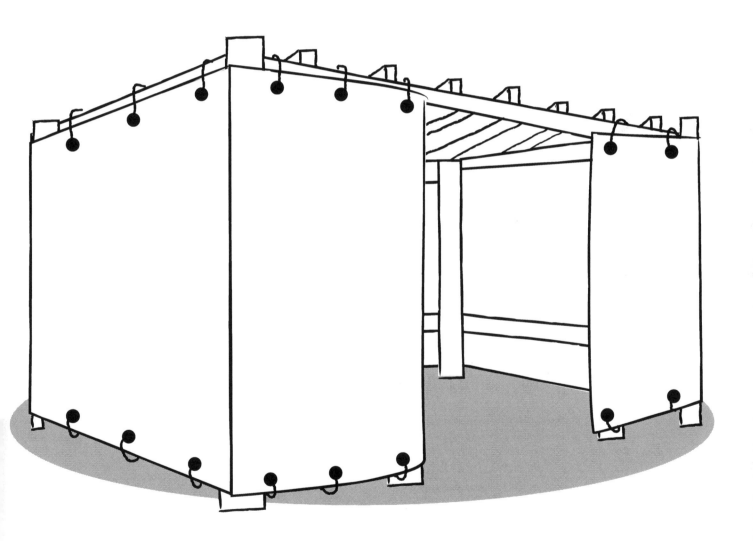

MARRIAGE SUPPER

Open your Bibles and read Revelation 19:7-8. Fill in the Blanks. Color the picture.

" Let us .... and exult

and give Him the ....,

for the .... of the

Lamb has come, and His

.... has made herself

ready; it was granted her to

clothe herself with fine linen,

bright and pure. "

REJOICE
GLORY
MARRIAGE
BRIDE

TEST YOUR SUKKOT KNOWLEDGE!

Read Leviticus 23, 1 Kings 8, Zechariah 14, John 1, Acts 18,
and Nehemiah 8. How much do you know about Sukkot?
Take this quiz to find out and share the results with your friends!

1. Which Feast did Yeshua secretly attend in John 1? ....

2. What did the Israelites do every day during Sukkot in Nehemiah 8? ....

3. Where did Solomon offer burnt offerings to Yah during Sukkot
   in 1 Kings 8? ....

4. For how many days do people honor Sukkot? ....

5. What did the Israelites live in during Sukkot? ....

6. What were the Israelites told to do on the first and seventh day
   of Sukkot? ....

7. In Zechariah 14, where will the people celebrate Sukkot? ....

8. How did Yah tell the Israelites to celebrate Sukkot in Leviticus 23:40? ....

9. How long were the Israelites told to honor Sukkot in Leviticus 23? ....

10. Why did Paul want to return to Jerusalem in Acts 18:21? ....

THE MILLENNIAL REIGN

Read Leviticus 23, Revelation 20, Isaiah 11, 65, Psalm 72,
Ezekiel 48, 2 Peter 3, and Zechariah 2.
Answer the questions below.

1. What are we instructed to do the eighth day of Sukkot? (Lev 23:36) ....

2. How long do followers of Yeshua reign with Him in the Millennial

    Reign? (Revelation 20:4) ....

3. Which animal will lie down with a goat? (Isaiah 11:6) ....

4. Which animal will feed with a cow? (Isaiah 11:7) ....

5. "With Yah, a day is like a ___ years and a thousand years are like a day." ....

6. "Then all ___ will be blessed through Him and they will call Him

    blessed." (Isaiah 65:13) ....

7. How big is the Levites allotment? (Ezekiel 48:13) ....

8. City workers will come from which tribes of Israel? (Ezekiel 48:19) ....

9. Who will be considered cursed? (Isaiah 65:20) ....

10. From which city will Yeshua rule the House of Israel? (Zechariah 2:12) ....

THE LAST GREAT DAY

Read Isaiah 11, Ezekiel 38-40, and Revelation 20.
Find and circle each of the words from the list below.

```
K A N G E L I L R E L N U N N G Y M O M
H E A V E N G X G M P Q M O E N W A N T
T L W Z I O D H C R F F I F Z Y Q N E B
H A G B N S X R T Y X W F S E H K A T U
O C B F K W W M A E D X I P K Y R S H Y
E Q P E L V G A R G X O W E I C N S O S
Y B X X R D C D Q L O R M L E J Y E U R
B X G F T N X H P C T N B A L T C H S A
J Q C H W A A A G B M X N C Q L A P A Q
U Q Q Q E Q J C E H P F R L A E B J N B
M M D M L Y Z N L S M C A E B V R O D Y
O A G I V L E R Q E X Y Q J G I T V Z W
T F I M E R T S P N S L I O N T B I S T
J T G C T Z O E H Z A R B G K E L M K H
Y C O B R A G Z M U N E B Y J S E E T R
R M G P I H L D R P A Q Z L O X Y D D O
O R Z Z B V E S D P L I R O N R O D R N
W I V R E L W N K E Y E D M M X S A W E
F C P H S L M J Q E M D A C Z J J C M G
S X J E R U S A L E M N G R P I U Q V L
```

DRAGON	COBRA	THRONE	ONE THOUSAND
TWELVE TRIBES	TEMPLE	JERUSALEM	HEAVEN
LION	MANASSEH	LEVITES	YESHUA
EZEKIEL	TABERNACLES	IRON ROD	ANGEL

LIFE IN THE MILLENNIAL REIGN

Read Isaiah 11, 34, 66, Psalm 72, Luke 22, and Ezekiel 48.
On the scrolls below, write four things that will be different about life in the Millennial Reign.

YESHUA WILL RULE

Read Revelation 20:1-6. Fill in the blanks below.

"I saw an angel coming out of ...., having the key to the Abyss and holding in his hand a great chain. He seized the dragon, that ancient serpent who is Ha'Satan, and tied him up for a thousand years. He threw him into the .... and locked and sealed it over him, to keep him from deceiving the nations until the 1000 years were ended. After that, he must be set free for a short time. I saw .... on which were seated those who had been given authority to judge. I saw the souls of those who had been beheaded because of their testimony of Yeshua and because of the Word of Yah. They had not worshiped the beast or its image and had not received its mark on their .... or their hands. They came to life and reigned with Yeshua for a .... years.   (The rest of the dead did not come to life until 1000 years were ended.) This is the first resurrection. Blessed and .... are those who share in the first .... The second death has no power over them, but they will be priests of Yah and ...., and reign with Him for a 1000 years. "

HEAVEN	FOREHEADS
ABYSS	YESHUA
THOUSAND	THRONES
RESURRECTION	HOLY

THE MILLENNIAL TEMPLE

Read Ezekiel 48. Use the diagram of Ezekiel's temple below to help you answer the quiz questions on the next page.

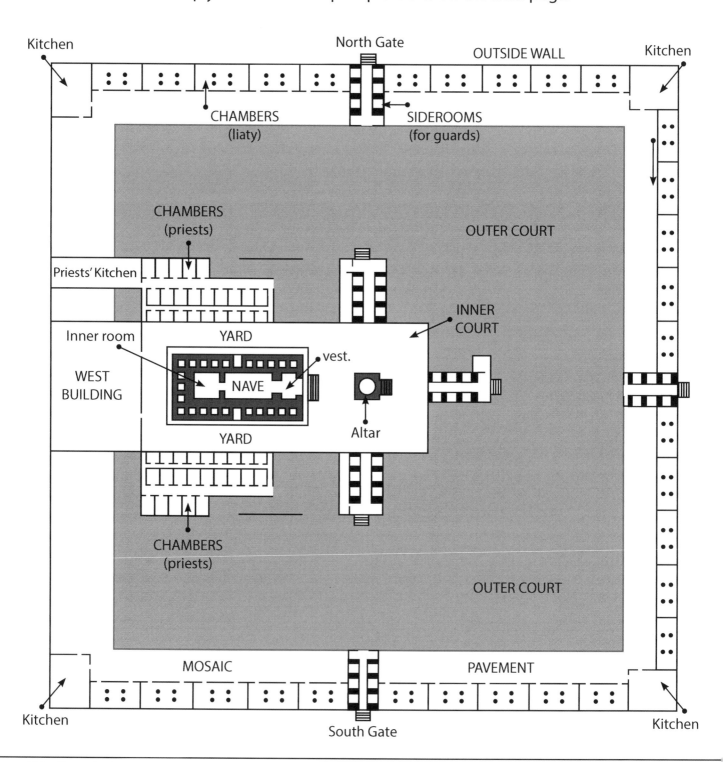

EZEKIEL'S TEMPLE

Read Ezekiel 40-44.
Answer the questions below.

1. To whom was Ezekiel instructed to share his vision?   ....

2. How many rooms were on either side of the East Gate?   ....

3. How big were the vestibules in the inner court?   ....

4. Where are the burnt, sin, and guilt offerings to be slaughtered?   ....

5. What was engraved on the inner temple walls? (Ezekiel 41:18)   ....

6. How many faces did each cherub have?   ....

7. Where shall the priests eat the holy offerings?   ....

8. What direction shall the steps of the altar face? (Ezekiel 43:17)   ....

9. Why shall the outer gate of the sanctuary remain shut?   ....

10. The temple priests are from which tribe of Israel?   ....

Shemini Atzeret

Read John 7:1-52. Write a short summary below.

....

....

....

1. Which Feast did Yeshua attend?

....

....

2. Where did Yeshua teach during this Feast?

....

....

3. What did Yeshua say to the crowd on the last day?

....

....

Draw your favorite scene from this story.

What could Shemini Atzeret teach me?	Yah used Yeshua to...

THE LAST GREAT DAY

Read the Bible verses below.
Write one or two sentences about Yah's message in each Bible verse.

Leviticus 23:26

"On the eighth day you shall hold a holy convocation and present a food offering to Yah. It is a solemn assembly; you shall not do any ordinary work."

....

....

Numbers 29:35

"On the eighth day you shall have a solemn assembly. You shall not do any ordinary work."

....

....

John 7:37-38

"On the last day of the feast, the great day, Yeshua stood up and cried out, "If anyone thirsts, let him come to Me and drink. Whoever believes in Me, as the Scripture has said, 'Out of his heart will flow rivers of living water."

....

....

JUDGING THE TWELVE TRIBES

Open your Bibles and read Matthew 19:28. Fill in the Blanks. Color the picture.

" I say to you, in the regeneration when the Son of .... sits on the .... of His glory, you who have followed Me will also sit on .... thrones, judging the twelve .... of Israel. "

MAN
GLORY
TWELVE
TRIBES

WHAT A LOT OF ANIMALS!

In the Millennial Reign, animals will live peacefully together.
Read Isaiah 11:6-8 and list eight animals that will live together. Color the pictures.

1. ....
2. ....
3. ....
4. ....
5. ....
6. ....
7. ....
8. ....

www.biblepathwayadventures.com
The Fall Feasts: Activity Book
© BPA Publishing Ltd 2019

EZEKIEL

Open your Bible to Ezekiel 39:25. Copy the scripture on the lines provided.
Use your imagination to color the illustration at the bottom of the page.

FEAST OF TABERNACLES

Read Zechariah 14:16-19. In the Millennial Reign, everyone must visit Jerusalem for the Feast of Tabernacles. Help an Israelite find his way to the Temple!

Last Great Day

Draw the Millennial temple.

I honor the Last Great Day by...

This Appointed Time teaches me...

If the Last Great Day was a book, the cover would look like this...

CRAFTS & PROJECTS

MAKE YOUR OWN SHOFAR

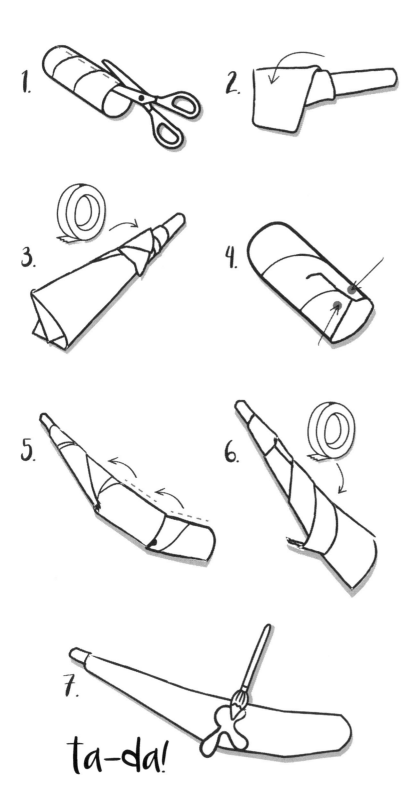

1.

2.

3.

4.

5.

6.

7.

ta-da!

You will need:

1. Three toilet rolls per shofar
2. A party horn
3. A paint brush
4. Brown and white paint
5. Masking tape
6. Scissors (adult only)
7. Extra-strength glue sticks or School glue

Instructions:

1. Use your scissors to cut lengthwise along one toilet roll.
2. Remove the plastic noise maker from a party horn. Wrap the cut cardboard tube around the plastic noisemaker.
3. Attach the cardboard roll to the plastic noisemaker with masking tape.
4. Take two more toilet rolls, fold the edge to make a pleat in the bottom side (the bottom should be small enough to fit inside another roll).
5. Place the folded toilet rolls inside each other.
6. Wrap the toilet paper rolls with masking tape
7. Paint your toilet roll shofar with white paint. While the white paint is still wet, add dashes of brown paint and mix to make your shofar look like a real shofar!

WHO SAID IT?

Read Matthew 24, Numbers 29, Judges 7, and Nehemiah 4.
Color and cut out each Bible character.
Match the quote with the person who said it.

1.
"He will send out His angels with a loud shofar blast and they will gather His elect…"
- Matthew 24:31

2.
"On the first day of the seventh month you shall have a set-apart time…It is a day for you to blow the shofars…"
- Numbers 29:1

3.
"When I blow the shofar, I and all who are with me then blow the shofar…"
- Judges 7:18

4.
"In the place where you hear the sound of the shofar, rally to us there. Yah will fight for us."
-Nehemiah 4:20

Moses   Gideon   Nehemiah   Yeshua

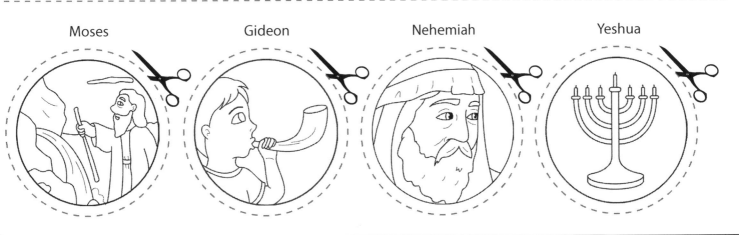

DAY OF TRUMPETS

Let's learn about the Day of Trumpets. Read Leviticus 23 and Numbers 29.
Cut out a sentence at the bottom of the page. Place it next to the correct picture.

Harvest time ✂

Seventh month ✂

Sabbath day ✂

Yah's people gather ✂

Blow the shofar ✂

WHO SAID IT?

Read Leviticus 16:6, Jonah 3-4, and Matthew 12:39.
Color and cut out each Bible character.
Match the quote with the person who said it.

1.

"A wicked and adulterous generation asks for a miraculous sign! But none will be given except the sign of the prophet, Jonah."
- Matthew 12:39

2.

"Let man and animal be covered with sackcloth and call out mightily to Yah…"
- Jonah 3:8

3.

"Aaron shall offer a bull as a sin offering for himself and make atonement for himself and his house."
- Leviticus 16:6

4.

"In forty days, Nineveh shall be overthrown!"
- Jonah 3:4

Jonah   King of Nineveh   Yahweh   Yeshua

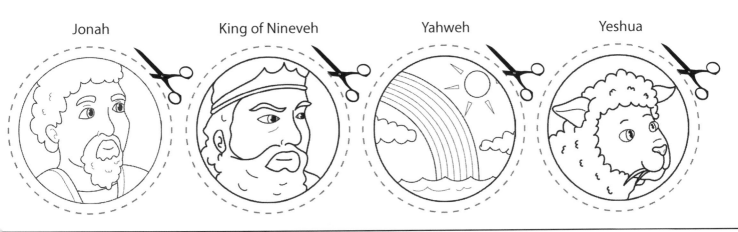

THE WATER CEREMONY

Every day during Sukkot, a priest took water from a special pool in Jerusalem to use in the temple. Cut out the objects. Place them in the picture.

Priest

Water

Jug

WHO SAID IT?

Read Deuteronomy 31, 1 Kings 8, John 14, and Nehemiah 8.
Color and cut out each Bible character.
Match the quote with the person who said it.

1.

"Whoever drinks of the water that I will give him will never be thirsty again…"
– John 4:14

2.

"Go out to the hills and bring branches of olive, wild olive, myrtle, palm, and other leafy trees to make booths."
- Nehemiah 8:15

3.

"Let your heart therefore be perfect with Yah, to walk in His statutes and keep His commandments…"
– 1 Kings 8:61

4.

"At the end of every seven years… at the Feast of Tabernacles when all Israel appears before Yah…you shall read this Torah…"
– Deuteronomy 31:10

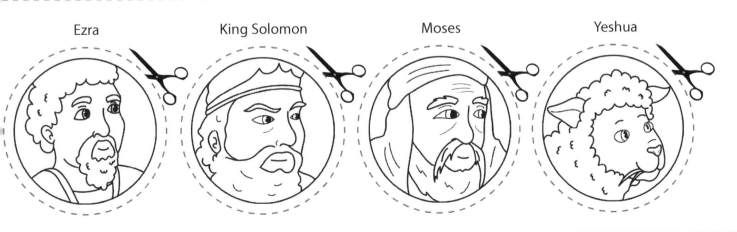

Ezra   King Solomon   Moses   Yeshua

ANSWER KEY

DAY OF TRUMPETS (Yom Teru'ah)
Day of Trumpets Word Search Puzzle

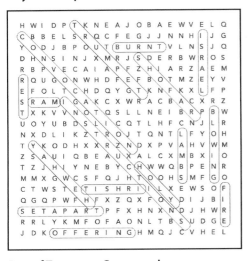

Day of Trumpets Crossword
Across
4) Seventh
5) Blowing
6) Shofar
8) Rest
9) Dead
10) Ram

Down
1) Yeshua
2) Yom Teru'ah
3) First
7) Food

Day of Trumpets Quiz
1. Tishri
2. A shofar (ram's horn)
3. No ordinary work
4. Month
5. One bull from the herd, one ram, seven male lambs a year old without blemish; also their grain offering of fine flour mixed with oil, three tenths of an ephah for the bull, two tenths for the ram, and one tenth for each of the seven lambs; with one male goat for a sin offering, to make atonement for you.

6. Grain offering
7. Israelites
8. Day of Atonement (Yom Kippur) and Tabernacles (Sukkot)
9. Israelites / people of Israel
10. The last 'trump'

Day of Trumpets: Color 'n Fill-in-the-blanks
Yah spoke to Moses, saying, "Speak to the people of Israel, saying, In the seventh month, on the first day of the month, you shall observe a day of solemn rest, a memorial proclaimed with blast of trumpets, a holy convocation. You shall not do any ordinary work, and you shall present a food offering to Yah."

Yom Teru'ah Word Scramble
1. Shofar
2. Yeshua
3. Day
4. Israelite
5. Set Apart
6. Blast
7. Yom Teru'ah
8. Blast

What's the Word?: The Last Trump
Behold! I tell you a mystery. We shall not all sleep, but we shall all be changed in a moment, in the twinkling of an eye, at the last trumpet. For the trumpet will sound, and the dead will be raised imperishable and we shall be changed.

DAY OF ATONEMENT (YOM KIPPUR)
Day of Atonement Quiz
1. Aaron
2. The holy linen coat, linen undergarment, the linen sash around his waist, and the linen turban
3. He washed himself
4. The goat was presented before Yah and then sent away into the wilderness
5. Over the mercy seat
6. People of Israel
7. No one
8. Moses
9. Tenth day of the seventh month
10. Rest and afflict ourselves

Day of Atonement Word Search Puzzle

Holy of Holies Word Search Puzzle

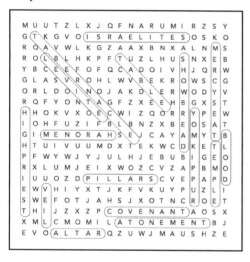

Fact Sheet: Repentance
1. To turn towards the Father and His Ways
2. To show Yah they had repented the Ninevites wore sackcloth. This was a coarse, black cloth made from goat's hair that was worn with burnt ashes as a sign of repentance.

Prayer of Repentance
Jonah prayed to Yah from the belly of the fish, saying, "I called out to Yah out of my distress, and He answered me. Out of the grave I cried and You heard my voice. You threw me into the sea and the waters surrounded me; Your powerful waves splashed over me. Then I said, 'I am driven away from Your sight; yet I will look again upon your holy temple.' The sea water closed over me to take my life. The deep surrounded me - seaweed wrapped around my head. I went down to the land whose

bars closed upon me forever; yet You brought up my life from the grave, Oh Yah my Elohim. When my life was fading away, I remembered Yah and prayed to You, into Your holy temple. Those who worship useless idols forsake their hope of steadfast love. But with thanks, I will sacrifice to You - what I have vowed I will pay. Salvation belongs to Yah!" Yah spoke to the fish and it vomited Jonah out upon the dry land.

Jonah and the Big Fish Quiz
1. Nineveh
2. Tarshish
3. Joppa
4. Yahweh sent a storm
5. Sailors
6. He was swallowed by a big fish
7. Three days and three nights
8. Prayed and cried out to Yahweh
9. God spoke to the fish and it vomited Jonah out onto dry land
10. To repent

Jonah and the Big Fish Word Search Puzzle

The High Priest Quiz
1. Aaron
2. Blue (Exo 28:31)
3. Day of Atonement (Yom Kippur)
4. Father-in-law (John 18:13)
5. Melchizedek
6. Annas (Luke 3:2)
7. Jehoiada (2 Chronicles 22:11)
8. Twelve
9. Abiathar (1 Kings 2:26)
10. Levi (1 Chronicles 6:4-8)

High Priest's Breastplate

Reuben, Simeon, Judah, Levi, Benjamin, Manasseh, Zebulun, Issachar, Gad, Dan, Naphtali, Asher

The Tabernacle

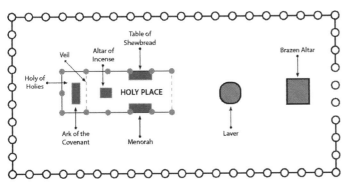

Fact Sheet: Holy of Holies

1. After the temple was built in Jerusalem, the High Priest would go inside a special room, called the Holy of Holies, and present an offering to Yah to symbolize the request from the Israelites for forgiveness.
2. Yeshua HaMashiach

Color 'n fill-in-the-blanks activity: Repentance

"But I declared first to those in Damascus, then in Jerusalem, and throughout Judea, and also to the nations that they should repent and turn to Yah, performing deeds in keeping with their repentance."

SUKKOT (TABERNACLES)
Sukkot Quiz

1. Forever – throughout the generations
2. Seven days, plus the Last Great Day
3. Sukkot (Tabernacles)
4. On the fifteenth day of the seventh month
5. Live in temporary dwellings and rejoice (a wedding celebration!)
6. Fall (Northern hemisphere), Spring (Southern hemisphere)
7. First and eighth day
8. The Israelites' exodus out of Egypt
9. King Solomon
10. No rain

Sukkot Word Search Puzzle

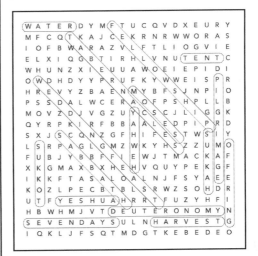

Fact Sheet: The Temple

1. To fit the large number of pilgrims coming to Jerusalem for Unleavened Bread, Shavuot, and Sukkot.
2. In the courtyards.
3. The highest court of Jewish law during the time of Roman rule.

King Solomon dedicates the Temple

1. Seventh month
2. They put the ark of the covenant in the Holy of Holies
3. He sacrificed 120,000 sheep and goats and 22,000 head of cattle.

Solomon's Temple diagram

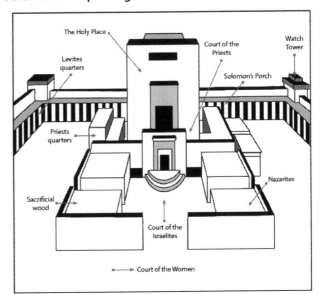

What's the Word? Celebration!

On the second day, the heads of fathers' houses of all the people, the priests and the Levites, came together to Ezra the scribe to study the words of the Torah. They found written in the Torah that Yah had commanded by Moses that the Israelites should dwell in booths during the feast of the seventh month, and that they should proclaim it in all their towns and in Jerusalem, "Go out to the hills and bring back branches of olive, wild olive, myrtle, palm, and other leafy trees to make booths, as it is written." So the people went out and brought them, and made booths for themselves, each on his roof, and in their courts and in the courts of the house of God, and in the square at the Water Gate and in the square at the Gate of Ephraim. And all the people who had returned from the captivity made booths and lived in them. From the days of Jeshua the son of Nun to that day, the people of Israel had not done so. And there was great rejoicing. Day by day, from the first day to the last day, Ezra read from the Torah. They kept the feast seven days, and on the eighth day there was a solemn assembly, according to the rule.

Sukkot Word Scramble

1. Moses
2. Booths
3. Offering
4. Water
5. Branches
6. Feast
7. Seven Days
8. Wedding

Marriage supper

"Let us rejoice and exult and give Him the glory, for the marriage of the Lamb has come, and His Bride has made herself ready; it was granted her to clothe herself with fine linen, bright and pure."

Test your Sukkot knowledge!

1. Tabernacles
2. Read the Torah
3. On the altar in the temple area
4. Seven
5. Sukkahs
6. No ordinary work
7. Jerusalem
8. With fruit, palm fronds, thick branches & river-willows
9. Forever
10. To keep one of Yah's Feasts

THE LAST GREAT DAY
The Millennial Reign Quiz

1. Rest (it's a Sabbath)
2. One thousand years
3. Leopard
4. A bear
5. Thousand
6. Nations
7. 25,000 cubits long and 10,000 cubits' wide
8. All tribes of Israel
9. Someone who does not live until they are 100 years' old
10. Jerusalem

The Last Great Day Word Search Puzzle

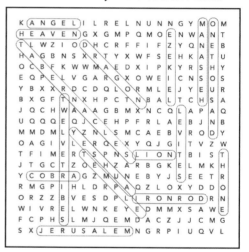

What's the Word?: Yeshua will rule!

I saw an angel coming out of heaven, having the key to the Abyss and holding in his hand a great chain. He seized the dragon, that ancient serpent who is Ha'Satan, and tied him up for a thousand years. He threw him into the Abyss and locked and sealed it over him, to keep him from deceiving the nations until the 1000 years were ended. After that, he must be set free for a short time. I saw thrones on which were seated those who had been given authority to judge. I saw the souls of those who had been beheaded because of their testimony of Yeshua and because of the Word of Yah. They had not worshiped the beast or its image and had not received its mark on their foreheads or their hands. They came to life and reigned with Yeshua for 1000 years. (The rest of the dead did not come to life until 1000 years were ended.) This is the first resurrection. Blessed and holy are those who share in the first resurrection. The second death has no power over them, but they will be priests of Yah and Yeshua, and reign with Him for a 1000 years.

Ezekiel's Temple Quiz
1. The House of Israel
2. Three side rooms
3. 25 cubits long and five cubits broad
4. In the vestibule of the gate
5. Cherubim and palm trees
6. Two faces
7. In the north and south chambers
8. East
9. Because the God of Israel has entered by it
10. Tribe of Levi

Shemini Atzeret worksheet
1. Feast of Tabernacles
2. The Temple
3. "If anyone thirsts, let him come to me and drink. Whoever believes in Me as the Scripture has said, 'Out of his heart will flow rivers of living water.'"

Fill-in-the-blanks and color: Judging the Twelve Tribes
I say to you, in the regeneration when the Son of Man sits on the throne of His glory, you who have followed Me will also sit on twelve thrones, judging the twelve tribes of Israel.

Coloring Activity: What a lot of animals!
Suggested answers
Wolf, lion, lamb, leopard, calf, cow, bear, cobra

Crafts & Projects
Page 87
Who said it?
1 = Yeshua, 2 = Moses, 3 = Gideon, 4 = Nehemiah

Page 91
Who said it?
1 = Yeshua, 2 = King of Nineveh, 3 = Yahweh, 4 = Jonah

Page 95
Who said it?
1 = Yeshua, 2 = Ezra, 3 = Solomon, 4 = Moses

◇ DISCOVER MORE ACTIVITY BOOKS! ◇

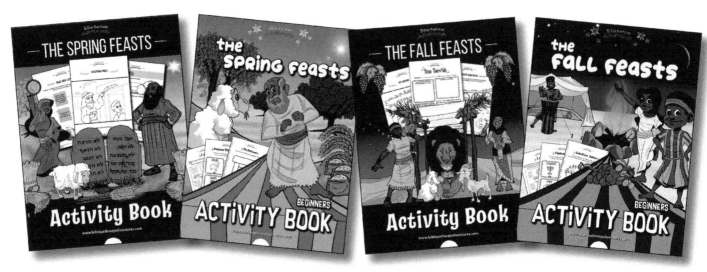

Available for purchase at www.biblepathwayadventures.com/store

INSTANT DOWNLOAD!

The Spring Feasts	Clean and Unclean
The Spring Feasts (Beginners)	Bereshit / Genesis
The Fall Feasts	Vayikra / Leviticus
Fall Feasts (Beginners)	Weekly Torah Portion

Made in the
USA
Columbia, SC